WE SHALL OVERCOME

THE LITTLE ROCK NINE

A PRIMARY SOURCE EXPLORATION OF THE BATTLE FOR SCHOOL INTEGRATION

by Brian Krumm

Consultant:
Bruce Allen Murphy, PhD
Fred Morgan Kirby Professor of Civil Rights
Lafayette College
Easton, Pennsylvania

CAPSTONE PRESS
a capstone imprint

Fact Finders are published by Capstone Press,
1710 Roe Crest Drive, North Mankato, Minnesota 56003
www.capstonepub.com

Library of Congress Cataloging-in-Publication Data
Krumm, Brian.
The Little Rock nine : a primary source exploration of the battle for school integration / by Brian Krumm.
pages cm.—(Fact finders. We shall overcome.)
Includes bibliographical references and index.
Summary: "Uses primary sources to tell the story of the Little Rock Nine during the U.S. Civil Rights Movement"—Provided by publisher.
ISBN 978-1-4914-0225-2 (library binding) — ISBN 978-1-4914-0234-4 (pbk.) — ISBN 978-1-4914-0230-6 (ebook PDF)
1. African Americans—Civil rights—Arkansas—Little Rock—History—20th century—Juvenile literature. 2. School integration—Arkansas—Little Rock—Juvenile literature. 3. Central High School (Little Rock, Ark.)—Juvenile literature. 4. Civil rights movements—Arkansas—Little Rock—History—20th century—Juvenile literature. 5. Civil rights workers—Arkansas—Little Rock—Biography—Juvenile literature. 6. Little Rock (Ark.)—Race relations—Juvenile literature. 7. African Americans—Civil rights—Arkansas—Little Rock—History—20th century—Sources.
I. Title.
F419.L7K78 2015
379.26309767'73—dc23 2013051317

Editorial Credits
Jennifer Besel, editor; Cynthia Akiyoshi, designer; Wanda Winch, media researcher;
Charmaine Whitman, production specialist

Photo Credits
AP Images, 22, 24; Atlanta Daily World, 19 (bottom); Birmingham, Alabama, Public Library Archives, File #1556.49.59, 9; Corbis: Bettmann, 27; Courtesy of Arkansas Democrat-Gazette, cover (bkgrnd); Courtesy of the Strom Thurmond Institute and Clemson University, 11; Courtesy of the Women's Emergency Committee to Open Our Schools, Morning Star Studio, 19 (top); Getty Images: Time Life Pictures/Ed Clark, 14, Time Life Pictures/Francis Miller, cover, 6, Time Life Pictures/Thomas D. McAvoy, 10, 15; Library of Congress: Prints and Photographs Division, 5, 12, 13, 17, 20, 28; Shutterstock: Olga k, paper background, Picsfive, paper pieces

Printed in the United States of America in Stevens Point, Wisconsin.
032014 008092WZF14

TABLE OF CONTENTS

A NOTE ABOUT PRIMARY SOURCES

Primary sources are newspaper articles, photographs, speeches, or other documents that were created during an event. They are great ways to see how people spoke and felt during that time. You'll find primary sources from the time of the Little Rock Nine school integration throughout this book. Within the text, primary source quotations are colored blue and set in italic type.

Chapter One

BRAVE DAYS

The windows of Central High School rattled with hateful shouts. An angry mob had gathered outside the school. Protesters screamed and threatened a small group of black students.

White protesters yelled at one student, *"**Lynch** her! Lynch her!"* Others spat at the students. The students' lives were in danger simply because they wanted to go to what had been an all-white school.

"As a child you don't process [it]," remembered Melba Pattillo, one of the black students there that day. When she saw the protesters, Pattillo remembers thinking, *"Why are they all here? Maybe there's going to be a parade? ... Slowly, it drips over you, like syrup ... I'm in the wrong place at the wrong time."*

lynch—to be put to death, often by hanging

▶ The Arkansas National Guard and hundreds of protesters crammed the streets and lawns around Central High School. The Guard wasn't there to control the crowd. Arkansas' governor had called the soldiers in to keep the black students out of the school.

▶ Taken on September 4, 1957, this photograph shows the powerful scene that unfolded in Little Rock that day. Soldiers made a barricade, blocking the African-American students from the school.

The mob and the group of black students it was trying to stop divided Little Rock, Arkansas, that September of 1957. A group of nine black students attempted to attend an all-white high school. The law was on the students' side. But the white community of Little Rock was not.

In the 1950s Arkansas and other states in the South were **segregated**. Laws forbade black and white people from eating, worshiping, or going to school together. And many white people wanted to keep it that way. White protesters often used violence to make their point. In 1957 some people threw a rock through an African-American woman's window. A note attached to the rock read, *"Stone This Time. Dynamite Next."*

But many people wanted to change the way African-Americans were treated. The black students who wanted to go to Central High School became known as the "Little Rock Nine." They were about to change history simply by attending school.

segregate—to keep people of different races apart in schools and other public places

Chapter Two

SEPARATE AND UNEQUAL

Years before the Little Rock Nine took center stage, African-Americans began fighting for equal rights. Slavery was **abolished** during the Civil War (1861–1865). But soon after the war, laws were put into place that segregated African-Americans. Especially in the South, black people did not have the same rights as white people. They were not allowed in many restaurants and hotels. They also had to use separate—and often broken-down—facilities. They were forced to ride in the backs of buses. And they were expected to give up their seats to white passengers if a bus was full.

African-Americans who did not follow the rules were fined or arrested. They lost their jobs. Many were attacked and even murdered.

abolish—to put an end to something officially

A Supreme Court case in 1896, *Plessy v. Ferguson,* made the unfair laws and treatment possible. The Supreme Court's decision in that case stated that it was legal to *"provide equal, but separate, accommodations for the white and [black] races."*

▶ Signs on segregated buses made it clear where black people were allowed to sit. Even if there were empty seats in the white section, African-Americans were forced to stand if their section was full.

A Major Ruling

Civil rights activists fought to get segregation laws overturned for years. In the 1930s activists turned their attention to education. Black and white schools all over the South were very unequal. Black schools often did not have reliable school buses or current textbooks. They also didn't have enough playground space or equipment for science classes.

The Supreme Court addressed this situation in the 1954 *Brown v. Board of Education* case. In the ruling Chief Justice Earl Warren wrote, *"in the field of public education, the doctrine of 'separate but equal' has no place. Separate educational facilities are inherently unequal."* The decision made **desegregation** mandatory in public schools.

▶ In many black schools, gym classes were held in hallways.

desegregation—getting rid of any laws or practices that separate people of different races

Angry with the ruling, white people formed groups to fight against **integration**. One hundred white Congress members signed "the Southern Manifesto." The document stated that the Supreme Court had no right to rule on state education policies. The document said, *"This unwarranted exercise of power by the Court ... is creating chaos and confusion ... It has planted hatred and suspicion where there has been ... friendship and understanding."*

Few African-Americans thought there had been much friendship and understanding.

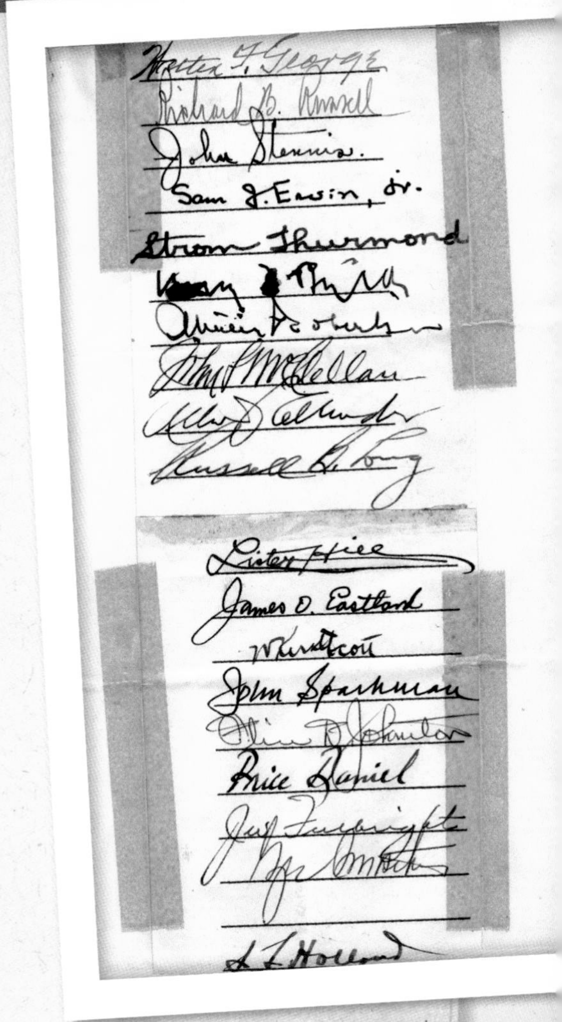

▶ In signing the Southern Manifesto, the lawmakers called the *Brown v. Board of Education* decision a *"clear abuse of judicial power."*

FACT

Supreme Court Justice Robert Jackson suffered a heart attack during the *Brown v. Board of Education* case. He was not expected to return to court. However, in a show of his support for the Court's decision, Jackson was there when the verdict was announced on May 17, 1954.

integration—the practice of including people of all races in schools and other public places

Making a Plan

The Supreme Court said all schools should take steps to integrate. The Little Rock school board came up with a plan in 1954. The school board decided that the high schools would integrate for the 1957–1958 school year. The junior high and elementary schools would follow later.

Integration would be an uphill battle. Even elected state officials promised to fight against it. Arkansas Governor Orval Faubus was one of them. Before he was elected governor, Faubus promised, *"No school district will be forced to mix the races as long as I am governor of Arkansas."*

▶ Arkansas governor Orval Faubus

▶ In September 1957, the Rev. Dr. Martin Luther King Jr. sent a telegram to President Dwight Eisenhower. In it he urged the president to *"take a strong forthright stand in the Little Rock situation."*

But many African-Americans felt strongly about working to end segregation. Civil rights leader Martin Luther King Jr. said, *"This is the ultimate tragedy of segregation. It not only harms one physically, but it injures one spiritually. It scars the soul and distorts the personality."*

Chapter Three

THE LITTLE ROCK NINE

After the Little Rock school board announced its integration plan, about 80 black students applied to attend Central High School. But many of those students were forced to reconsider. Business owners told black employees they would lose their jobs if their children tried to attend Central. By the winter of 1955–1956, just 33 black students were willing to attend white schools.

▶ Superintendent Virgil Blossom was not against integrating the Little Rock schools. But Blossom's plan to integrate the schools called for a slow process, starting with elementary students. Almost no one liked his original plan. African-American leaders said his plan was a delay tactic. And the school board preferred to start with high school students.

But the threats continued. Superintendent Virgil Blossom told black students they would face incredible stress. He also said they would not be able to participate in sports teams, bands, or clubs. *"[Blossom said] you're not going to be able to go to the football games or basketball games. You're not going to be able to participate in the choir or drama club, or be on the track team. You can't go to the prom,"* reported Carlotta Walls, a student who became one of the Little Rock Nine.

Regardless of Blossom's warnings, 10 students were chosen to integrate Central. Little did they know that soldiers would have to bring them to their classes.

NAACP

The National Association for the Advancement of Colored People (NAACP) was founded in 1909 to fight racism. The NAACP began taking legal action in the 1930s. Its lawyers played a big role in getting the *Brown v. Board of Education* case reviewed by the Supreme Court.

Daisy Bates was the Arkansas chapter president. She helped choose the students who would integrate Central High School. She and other NAACP members also provided support to the students and their families.

▶Arkansas NAACP chapter president Daisy Bates

The Students

Ten students were selected to integrate Central High School. Ernest Green was the only 12th grader in the group. Terrance Roberts, Elizabeth Eckford, Minnijean Brown, Thelma Mothershed, Gloria Ray, and Melba Pattillo were in 11th grade. Jefferson Thomas, Carlotta Walls, and Jane Hill were 10th graders. Hill decided to attend another school after the students' first attempt to enter Central on September 4. That left nine students to continue the fight for integration.

The students had good reason for wanting to attend Central. They knew that a **diploma** from Central, a highly respected school, could lead to college or better jobs. Ernest Green said later in life, *"We wanted to widen options for ourselves and later for our children."*

But while the students were preparing to integrate, other people were gearing up to stop it.

diploma—a certificate from a school that shows you have finished a course of study

▶ the Little Rock Nine along with NAACP chapter president Daisy Bates
back row (left to right): Jefferson Thomas, Melba Pattillo, Terrance Roberts, Carlotta Walls, Daisy Bates, and Ernest Green
front row (left to right): Thelma Mothershed, Minnijean Brown, Elizabeth Eckford, and Gloria Ray

Fighting Integration

Organizations in Little Rock formed to fight integration. The Mothers' League of Central High School was made up of mothers of white Central students. Mary Thomason, secretary of the League, filed a lawsuit in a local court to stop integration. She **testified** in court that she had heard rumors *"that there was a possibility of shotguns or shooting in Central High if [black students] entered."* Governor Faubus also testified in the case. He said there would be *"rioting and bloodshed."* Eventually, the lawsuit was dismissed.

However, the organizations vowed to keep fighting. Amis Guthridge, a lawyer for the Capital Citizens' Council, said, *"we will continue to fight in a peaceful manner to maintain the high principles upon which our Southern society was founded."* Guthridge meant that the group would fight to keep things segregated. But the fight would be anything but peaceful.

testify—to state facts in court

▶ This flyer was created by The Mothers' League of Central High School in 1958 to persuade voters to elect school board members who supported segregation.

DO YOU WANT NEGROES IN OUR SCHOOLS?

IF YOU DO NOT THEN GO TO THE POLLS THIS COMING MONDAY AND

VOTE

FOR REMOVAL	AGAINST REMOVAL
LAMB	McKINLEY
MATSON	ROWLAND
TUCKER	LASTER

THIS IS THE SIMPLE TRUTH. IF THE INTEGRATIONISTS WIN THIS SCHOOL BOARD FIGHT, THE SCHOOLS WILL BE INTEGRATED THIS FALL. THERE WILL BE ABSOLUTELY NOTHING YOU OR WE CAN DO TO STOP IT.

PLEASE VOTE RIGHT!!!

Join hands with us in this fight— send your contributions to

THE MOTHERS' LEAGUE

P. O. BOX 3321 • LITTLE ROCK, ARKANSAS

Ad Paid for by Margaret C. Jackson, President; Mary Thomason, Secretary

Dr. King Asks Non-Violence In Little Rock School Crisis

Dr. Martin Luther King, Jr., president of the Montgomery, Ala., Improvement Association, has urged the people of Little Rock, Ark, to be Christian and dignified in their struggle for integration and to fight violence with non-violence.

Dr. King's message was sent by telegram to Mrs. L. C. Bates, president of the NAACP at Little Rock, and the Rev. Roland Smith, prominient Negro minister in that city according to a spokesman for the association.

DIFFICULT ADVICE

Dr. King renown pastor of Dexter Avenue Baptist Church in Montgomery, said:

"Urge the people of Little Rock to adhere rigorously to a way of non-violence at this time. I know this is difficult advice at a time when you are being terrorized, stoned, and threatened by ruthless mobs. But non-violence is the only way to a lasting solution of the problem.

"You must meet physical force with soul force. You have no alternative but to continue the struggle for integrated schools, but do it with a thorough committnient to Christian principles. If the white mobs of Little Rock choose to be un-Christian and disgracefully barbaric in their acts, you must continue to be Christian and dignified in yours.

MOB RULE

"History is on your side. World opinion is with you. The moral conscience of millions of white Americans is with you. Keep struggling with this faith and the tragic midnight of anarchy and mob rule which encompasses your city at this time will be transformed into the glowing daybreak of freedom and justice."

LAST ATTEMPTED

Referring to Gov. Orval Faubus' calling out the Arkansas National Guard on Sept., 2 apparently to impede integration processes, Dr King recently termed this "a last desperate attempt of the South to delay integration at all costs."

The young minister has said he is "optismistic' 'about the integration process and has predicted that "before the turn of the century segregation and discrimination will not exist in America."

▶ As the fight heated up, King and other civil rights leaders worried the students would be attacked. But King urged civil rights activists to remain nonviolent, as reported in this September 26, 1957, article from the *Atlanta Daily World*.

Chapter Four

GETTING IN

On September 4, 1957, the black students arrived at Central. A mob greeted them with spit and screams. But it wasn't the mob that kept the students out of school. Governor Faubus had ordered the National Guard to keep the students out. Faubus claimed that, *" ... it will not be possible ... to maintain order and protect the lives and property of the citizens if forcible integration is carried out ..."*

The school board then asked a court to delay integration. The students didn't return to school until September 23. That day about 1,000 protesters gathered in front of Central. The students made their way through the threatening crowd.

Elizabeth Eckford's family didn't have a telephone. So she did not know the other eight black students were going to school together. Eckford arrived at the school alone and was confronted by the mob. This iconic photograph shows Hazel Bryan screaming at Eckford.

A newspaper report from the next day described the events.

"The crowd now let out a roar of rage. 'They've gone in!' a man shouted ...

"A group of six girls ... started to shriek and wail ...

"Hysteria swept from the shrieking girls to ... the crowd. ...

"By 12 o'clock the mob had reached its greatest strength, and by now completely ignored the local police. The crowd remained behind the barricade, but it did not maintain order there. Several newsmen were attacked and beaten. A Negro reporter was kicked and manhandled.

"Threats, jeers, and insults became more ominous ..."

Finally, an officer made an announcement. At about noon he said the black students had been removed from the school.

Later in life Gloria Ray said that the students left Central after only a few hours because of the mob outside. For Ray it was *"the most horrifying experience I've had in my life ... You could hear the noise from the mob, and it was getting louder and louder and louder ... Then at a certain point the noise from the mob was not quite as loud as the thumping of my own heart ..."*

A City in Crisis

The situation in Little Rock was out of control. President Dwight Eisenhower had been watching the events at Central closely. After the dangerous scene of September 23, school officials told the Little Rock Nine not to come to school the next day. Eisenhower took action.

"I will use the full power of the United States, including whatever force may be necessary ... to carry out the orders of the federal court," Eisenhower said in an announcement to the nation. On September 24, about 1,200 U.S. Army troops took up positions around Central High School. The next morning they brought the Little Rock Nine to school.

Minnijean Brown was overcome with emotion. The fact that the president took action so she could attend school had a powerful impact on her. *"For the first time in my life,"* she said, *"I feel like an American citizen."*

But other people in Little Rock felt their rights were being ignored. Faubus said, *"My fellow citizens, we are now an occupied territory ... what is happening in America?"*

▶ Soldiers from the 101st Airborne Division stood guard outside Central with rifles and bayonets. Their orders were to protect the Little Rock Nine and make sure they could go to school.

Chapter Five

JUST THE BEGINNING

Crowds continued to protest at Central every day. The people shouted sayings such as *"Two, four, six, eight, we ain't gonna integrate"* at the Little Rock Nine. Inside the school each of the Little Rock Nine was verbally and physically attacked. Ernest Green said going to school *"was like going into battle every day."*

Crowds of white men and women surrounded Central for weeks. Each day soldiers had to escort the Little Rock Nine into school to protect them from the crowds.

Some white students did try to be friendly to the black students. Robin Woods, a white Central student said, *"I got integrated yesterday. That was the first time I'd ever gone to school with a Negro, and it didn't hurt a bit."*

Central's student newspaper, *The Tiger,* ran many editorials on the topic of integration. Editor Jane Emery wrote, *"The challenge is yours, as future adults of America, to prove your maturity, intelligence, and ability to make decisions by how you react, behave, and conduct yourself ..."*

An Apology

Several years after Central was integrated, Elizabeth Eckford received a phone call. On the other end was Hazel Bryan—the woman who had been captured screaming at Eckford in that famous photo. Bryan apologized for her actions during the event.

A Long Year

The violence and attacks continued throughout the school year. Minnijean Brown was **expelled** from Central for standing up to her bullies. Before she was expelled, she said, *"I don't think people realize what goes on at Central ... They throw rocks, they spill ink on your clothes ... they just keep bothering you every five minutes."*

Sammie Dean, a Central student, said he didn't think the poor treatment would stop. *"The South has always been against racial mixing,"* Dean said. *"I think they will fight this thing to the end."*

But none of the Little Rock Nine quit. On May 27, 1958, Ernest Green became the first African-American graduate of Central High. Almost no one in the audience clapped when he received his diploma. But it didn't matter to him. *"Nobody clapped. But I figured they didn't have to. Because after I got that diploma, that was it. I had accomplished what I had come there for."*

expel—to force a student to leave school

Jefferson Thomas and Elizabeth Eckford pictured in the Central High lunchroom on October 10, 1957.

FACT

Martin Luther King Jr. attended Ernest Green's graduation ceremony to show his support.

Never Giving Up

Faubus and his supporters continued to fight against school integration. In August 1958 Arkansas lawmakers passed a law allowing the governor to close schools. The next month the Supreme Court made another landmark ruling in *Cooper v. Aaron*. The ruling said that decisions made by the Court must be followed by all states. To avoid following the decision, Faubus closed all public high schools in Little Rock. On September 12, 1958, Faubus announced, *"... I have ordered closed the senior high schools of Little Rock, in order to avoid the impending violence and disorder which would occur and to preserve the peace of the community."*

▶ This sign was put up outside Central. Its message was incorrect, however. The federal government did not close the school. Arkansas' governor ordered the closure.

In June 1959 a federal court ruled that closing the schools was unconstitutional. In August the schools reopened. At the end of the school year, Jefferson Thomas and Carlotta Walls graduated from Central.

"It became ... important to graduate because ... I had to prove something to myself that I wouldn't cave or give in under stress or adversity," Thomas later said.

It wasn't until 1972 that all Little Rock public schools were integrated. By that time each of the Little Rock Nine had attended college and was leading a successful life. Because of their bravery, they had changed a nation. They continue to serve as inspiration for others who want to change unfair conditions. These pioneers made an incredible impact through dedication, strength, and sacrifice.

FACT

President Bill Clinton awarded each of the Little Rock Nine the Congressional Gold Medal in 1998. The medal shows appreciation for citizens' outstanding achievements.

Selected Bibliography

Brown v. Board of Education of Topeka, Opinion; May 17, 1954; Records of the Supreme Court of the United States; Record Group 267; National Archives.

Chadwick, Alex. "Little Rock Remembers Troops' Arrival." NPR, September 24, 2007. http://www.npr.org/templates/story/story.php?storyId=14654126

"Choices People Made: Legacies." Facing History and Ourselves website. https://www.facinghistory.org/for-educators/educator-resources/resource-collections/choosing-to-participate/choices-people-made-legacies

Emery, Jane. "Can You Meet the Challenge?" *The Tiger,* September 19, 1957. http://www.ncdemocracy.org/sites/www.ncdemocracy.org/files/docs/NDEP-LittleRock-STUDENT_EDITORIALS.pdf

Fine, Benjamin. "Militia Sent to Little Rock; School Integration Put Off." *The New York Times,* September 3, 1957. http://events.nytimes.com/learning/general/specials/littlerock/090357ds-militia.html

Fine, Benjamin. "President Threatens to Use U.S. Troops, Orders Rioters in Little Rock to Desist; Mob Compels 9 Negroes to Leave School." *The New York Times,* September 24, 1957. http://events.nytimes.com/learning/general/specials/littlerock/092457ds-prexy.html

"The Little Rock Nine: 50 Years Later" *The New York Times* Interactive Graphic. http://www.nytimes.com/interactive/2007/10/01/us/20071001_LITTLEROCK_GRAPHIC.html?_r=0

Plessy vs. Ferguson, Judgement, Decided May 18, 1896; Records of the Supreme Court of the United States; Record Group 267; Plessy v. Ferguson, 163, #15248, National Archives.

Sitton, Claude. "Court Bars Little Rock Delay; President Calls For Support; Faubus Orders 4 Schools Shut." *The New York Times,* September 13, 1958. http://events.nytimes.com/learning/general/specials/littlerock/091358ds-court.html

Washington, James M., ed. *A Testament of Hope: The Essential Writings and Speeches of Martin Luther King Jr.* New York: HarperCollins, 1991.

Glossary

abolish (uh-BOL-ish)—to put an end to something officially

desegregation (dee-seg-ruh-GAY-shuhn)—getting rid of any laws or practices that separate people of different races

diploma (duh-PLOH-muh)—a certificate from a school that shows you have finished a course of study

expel (ik-SPEL)—to force a student to leave school

integration (in-tuh-GRAY-shuhn)—the practice of including people of all races in schools and other public places

lynch (LYNCH)—to be put to death, often by hanging, by mob action and without legal authority

segregate (SEG-ruh-gate)—to keep people of different races apart in schools and other public places

testify (TESS-tuh-fye)—to state facts in court

Critical Thinking Using the Common Core

1. How did President Dwight Eisenhower affect the civil rights movement by sending troops to guard the Little Rock Nine? (Key Ideas and Details)

2. Compare the quotations from Minnijean Brown and Governor Orval Faubus on page 23. Explore how these two quotations show the different points of view surrounding school integration in the South. (Craft and Structure)

Internet Sites

FactHound offers a safe, fun way to find Internet sites related to this book. All of the sites on FactHound have been researched by our staff.

Here's all you do:
Visit *www.facthound.com*
Type in this code: 9781491402252

Index